UNCREATED GOD

by Jacob and Sara Haywood
illustrated by George Scondras

REASON FOR HOPE

Text Copyright © 2021 Jacob and Sara Haywood
Illustrations Copyright © 2021 George Scondras

All rights reserved. No part of this book may be reproduced or used
in any manner without the prior written permission of the copyright owner,
except for the use of brief quotations in a book review.

To request permissions, contact the publisher at info@reasonforhopeministries.com.

All scripture quotations are from the Holy Bible, New Living Translation,
copyright © 1996, 2004, 2007 by Tyndale House Foundation.
Used by permission of Tyndale House Publishers, Inc., Carol Stream, IL 60188.
All rights reserved.

Hardcover: 978-1-955108-01-0
Paperback: 978-1-955108-00-3
E-Book: 978-1-955108-02-7

Reason for Hope, LLC
Tullahoma, TN

reasonforhopeministries.com

They know the truth about God because he has made it obvious to them. For ever since the world was created, people have seen the earth and sky. Through everything God made, they can clearly see his invisible qualities—his eternal power and divine nature. So they have no excuse for not knowing God.

— Romans 1:19-20 —

Long before there was anything...
Way before there was everything...

There was NOTHING.

But...

GOD

was.

He was before anything,
and He was everything's CAUSE.

God the FATHER, God the SON, and God the SPIRIT always were.

Together they formed creation.

It was not an accident that just occurred.

from the birds
in the trees
to the angels
watching over
you and me.

UNTOUCHABLE...

God formed man with His own hands.

In His image He made us to love sunshine and smiles, imagination and friends.

The Father sent the Son to pay the price.

Though we turned from Him,
He will forgive our sins,
if we trust in Jesus who is ALIVE.

UNSHAKABLE...

God will always be seated on His throne.

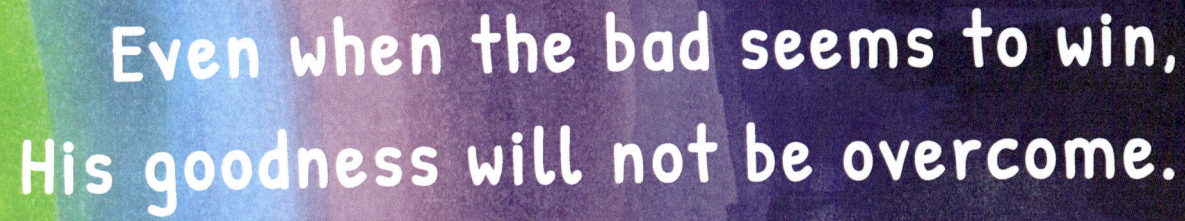

Even when the bad seems to win,
His goodness will not be overcome.

There are other stories about the beginning, but you can know this one is TRUE.

Long before you ever had a thought, God thought of YOU.

If God was not in the
BEGINNING
then nothing could ever be.

PARENT PAGE
DIVE DEEPER

Uncreated God is a simple, meaningful and beautiful book that can be used to introduce God's creation narrative to children. It can also be used for much more, specifically in teaching children how to defend the existence of God or even beginning the journey of apologetics for yourself!

Uncreated God is loosely based on the Cosmological Argument, which is generally used to convince those who are not believers in God that the existence of God, or at least some sort of "cause" of the universe, is both rational and necessary. The argument can be stated this way:
      1) Everything that has a beginning has a cause.
      2) The universe had a beginning.
      3) Therefore, the universe had a cause.

Although the Cosmological Argument is the primary framework of this book, we go beyond its bounds, as we are unashamed believers in the Christian God of the Bible. Revelation of God through His Word and creation informs us that God is the cause of everything that exists. This book, as well as Christian apologetics, defends that claim.

While the Cosmological Argument is a broad concept for kids (and even some adults) to understand, it is important to begin teaching theological truths about God at a young age so that when children are older, they can study and learn to defend them for themselves. Many children who have grown up in Bible-believing homes and churches will most likely know the creation story, but this book takes it a bit further to defend biblical truth against other alternative stories the world teaches.

Below are some talking points, artistic insights, and biblical references to give you a deeper understanding of creation in order for you to better present your child with the concepts of this book. Each point corresponds to the same page number in the book so you can easily look back and dive deeper every time you read it.

1. Scientists not so long ago thought the universe was eternal, therefore it did not need a cause to come into existence. Around the time of Albert Einstein, that all changed by several discoveries, including Einstein's theory of general relativity. His theory suggested that **there was a beginning to the universe**, and several scientific discoveries since then confirmed his theory.[1] How the beginning happened still continues to be debated among scientists and theologians, but for even more reasons than those presented in this book, we believe the biblical creation account is the true description of reality. *(Genesis 1:1)*

2. Much of the scientific community today believe there was at first nothing, then something came from nothing by means of what is called a singularity. This sort of "scientific" belief suggests, *"The universe began with every speck of its energy jammed into a very tiny point. This extremely dense point exploded with unimaginable force, creating matter and propelling it outward to make the billions of galaxies of our vast universe. Astrophysicists dubbed this titanic explosion the Big Bang."*[2] One of the largest problems with this theory is that **there was not actually nothing**, for where did *"every speck of its energy"* come from? Christian theology claims that God created out of nothing (*ex nihilo*). *(John 1:1-3)*

3. God has always existed for eternity past. Many kids often ask a question along the lines of, "But who created God?" If God was created, then who created that being, and so on and so forth? There has to be a starting point. **Something has to be eternal.** Since there was nothing in terms of material things, what else was there? There was God. God, as long defined by the Bible, is timeless, all-present and spirit, therefore can exist outside and before the time-space-material universe. He is also defined as all-powerful, therefore able to bring about the existence of all things. *(Revelation 1:8)*

(The Sierpiński triangles pictured on this page are a great way to teach your child about the notion of infinity or eternity. After counting the individual large triangles, ask your child to count the triangles within the triangles. The division represented in the triangles could be repeated an infinite amount of times, showing how long God has existed for eternity past.)

4. This page uses the word "cause" in reference to the philosophical notion of the first cause, meaning **there had to be an initial cause of all things**. If you glance back at the first point of the Cosmological Argument, you will see that *"everything that has a beginning has a cause."* Science is a study of cause and effect. There had to be a cause for the something to come from the nothing. **God is the cause.** He decided, out of His loving-kindness, to create. And boy, aren't we all glad that the He did? *(Colossians 1:16-17)*

5. The Christian notion of the Trinity is that **God is one in three persons**. Each person of the Trinity is co-equal and co-eternal and has always existed together in perfect, loving community. Though this is outside of our reasoning (which we should expect God to be), it is not against reason. Saying God is three *and* one would be against reason. God is three *in* one. *(Genesis 1:1-2; John 1:1-3)*

(On this page, the three primary colors of light—red, green, and blue—overlap each other within the Trinitarian symbol. When the primary colors of light are combined, white forms at the center. Page 5 shows God's creation displayed in the center of the colors/shapes of the Trinity, where everything is in perfect harmony.)

6. The scientific world that embraces evolution believes everything we see has come about essentially by time and chance. If nothing actually existed, the chance accident that began all things would literally be a supernatural miracle. However those who hold this view tend to believe that the supernatural and miracles are impossible. **It is contradictory to believe in a supernatural accident yet rule out a supernatural God.** *(Hebrews 11:3)*

7. The Unmoved Mover is a philosophical argument that dates back to Aristotle (384–322 BC). He argued that there had to be a "prime mover" or first "uncaused cause" of all the motion in the universe (think of the finger that pokes the first domino that then topples the next domino, and on and on and on). **If the Big Bang is true from natural forces, then what caused the bang? Where did the motion originate from?** The Bible reveals that it was God. *(Revelation 4:11)*

8. Another theological argument for God's existence is the Teleological Argument, which is the argument from design. Within it is a notion called the anthropic principle. "Anthropic" comes from the Greek word *anthropos*, meaning human. This principle shows us the incredible complexity of the universe and human life and argues that **the universe seems to be "finely tuned" to allow human life on earth.** This could not have happened by chance, but must have a Designer behind it. *(Psalm 104:5)*

9. The great philosopher, theologian, and Catholic priest, Thomas Aquinas (1225–1274 AD), took Aristotle's notion of the Unmoved Mover (from #7) further and applied it to Christianity. Aquinas' Uncreated Creator reveals that Aristotle's Unmoved Mover is indeed the God of Christianity, as presented in the Bible. Just like something in motion has to be set in motion, **only an uncreated being could create the first created thing**. *(Colossians 1:16-17)*

10. The nature of God's creation is broader than anyone can see or imagine. **God created the entire physical and spiritual realm and everything in it.** This includes everything you see when you look out the window as well as the unseen reality of spiritual beings and heaven and hell. *(Psalm 148:2–5)*

11. The Bible reveals that God made the first man and woman with His own hands and breathed into them His very own breath. He is personal. He is caring. He is creative. **Though He is so far beyond us in every way, He has humbled Himself and come near.** *(Genesis 2:7; 21-22)*

12. God created man and woman in His own image, different from all the rest of creation. There are several *"communicable attributes"* that God shares with us, meaning there are many characteristics of Himself that He has placed in mankind. Creativity, thinking, imagination, compassion, and relational love are some characteristics God shares with us. The image of God in humanity is why we are to treat each other nicely and to hold all life as sacred and important. *(Genesis 1:27, 5:1)*

13. God is unrelenting, or always passionately pursuing the salvation of sinners since the beginning of time. He chose to take on the form of man (Jesus) to be able to relate to us and save us. He had it planned before the creation of the world *(John 3:16; 1 Peter 3:18)*. 1 Peter 1:19-21 says, *"It was the precious blood of Christ, the sinless, spotless Lamb of God. God chose him as your ransom long before the world began, but now in these last days he has been revealed for your sake. Through Christ you have come to trust in God. And you have placed your faith and hope in God because he raised Christ from the dead and gave him great glory."*

14. The death that God the Son, Jesus, died on the cross, and His resurrection from the dead are the only means by which you and I can be saved from our sins. Romans 5:8 says, *"God showed his great love for us by sending Christ to die for us while we were still sinners."* And Romans 10:9, *"If you openly declare that Jesus is Lord and believe in your heart that God raised him from the dead, you will be saved."* **Have you placed your faith in Jesus?** If not, you can and should right now. Please visit **salvation.reasonforhopeministries.com.**

15. The Bible, in both the Old and New Testaments, reveals God as not just the Creator of the cosmos but also the King of the cosmos. He is the Ruler and Sustainer of all *(Isaiah 6:1-3; Colossians 1:17; Revelation 5)*. **God being "unshakable" is in direct contrast to our weakness and tendency to doubt, fear and fall.** There are many times in life where the truth of God's power and control is a comfort, especially when it seems like the world around us is crashing down. *(Ephesians 1:19-23; 2 Corinthians 12:9-10)*

16. The philosophical notion of the Problem of Evil—why bad things happen—is a common objection to the existence of God by many. There are numerous reasons as to why and how a good God could allow evil and suffering. One is that free creatures (humans and spiritual beings) over thousands of years have made choices that negatively affect many aspects of the world and our lives. But there are infinite goods that outweigh all the evils that exist. An infinite good is the incarnation and atonement of Jesus, which is God becoming man and dying for our sins.[3] Without the suffering of Jesus on the cross *(the Lamb that was slain—Revelation 5:6)* there would not be eternal life for mankind. **His demonstration of love through sacrifice and resurrection defeats evil and sin for all eternity.** *(Romans 8:37-39; John 16:33; 1 John 3:16)*

17. The prevalent scientific theory about creation that is most widely circulated in the world is Darwinian evolution, as the pictures on this page depict. Though Darwin's research only showed how animals could adapt, not completely change into different animals, his theory assumed a single beginning to all of life, one that was not *"intelligently designed."* Though Darwinism is a theory, it is taught as if it is a fact, even with a severe lack of observable evidence that evolution of a change of kinds has occurred. **It is far more reasonable that an intelligent being (God), created all things as the Bible has long revealed.** And there is much evidence of that truth, as this book argues a small portion of that evidence. *(Romans 1:19-20)*

(Multiple creation myths are presented on this page, including the lotus flower representing a variety of Eastern creation stories, water symbolizing ancient chaos myths of creation, and evolution progressing through time since the Big Bang. These myths are depicted to communicate that the Truth of the Bible is superior to tradition, superstition, and even scientific theory.)

18. God did not just create the universe to spin and move and exist in its splendor. No, He also created you to be a part of it. You are not a chance accident, as evolution argues. The Bible says you are fearfully and wonderfully made. **Before you were formed in your mother's womb, you were formed in the beautiful, creative imagination of God.** *(Psalm 139:13-14; Jeremiah 1:5)*

19. This is a recap and summary of the argument we have made. If not God, then who? Then what? **If God was not in the beginning, not a single thing would or could be.** *(John 1:1-3; Colossians 1:16-17)*

20. We can know God exists in two ways: through special revelation and general revelation. Special revelation is the Bible, God's very words. It is how we know things about Him, and most importantly, how to be saved. We can also know about God through general revelation, which is by looking at the world around us. **Mountains, sunsets, babies being born, and stars being formed all teach us of God's existence through His creation.** Even though we can't see Him with our eyes, we see the effects of His work all around us. *(Psalm 19:1-2; Romans 1:19-20)*

In addition to reading the creation story, **pointing out evidences of God's handiwork in nature will shape the way your children view God and the world around them.** Next time you are at the park, marvel over the trees and flowers and chirping birds. When you are on vacation at the beach, talk about the vastness and depth of the ocean compared with the intricate design of a seashell—God made them both! When you are camping with your family, look up at the stars and point out how great God must be to know them all by name.

God is real. It is evident in so many ways all around you. We hope you and your children cling to this truth and defend it amidst a world that claims a different narrative. To learn more about the existence of God and find hope in a hopeless world, please visit **reasonforhopeministries.com**.

1. Norman L. Geisler and Frank. Turek, *I Don't Have Enough Faith to Be an Atheist* (Wheaton, Ill: Crossway Books, 2004). See the scientific discoveries in Chapter 3 within the acronym SURGE.
2. https://www.exploratorium.edu/origins/cern/ideas/bang.html
3. Alvin Plantinga, "Supralapsarianism, or 'O Felix Culpa,'" in *Christian Faith and the Problem of Evil* (Grand Rapids: William B. Eerdmans, 2004).

www.ingramcontent.com/pod-product-compliance
Lightning Source LLC
Chambersburg PA
CBRC090910230426
43673CB00018B/425